Superbike Racing

by Ed Youngblood

Consultant:
Hugh Fleming
Director, AMA Sports
American Motorcyclist Association

CAPSTONE BOOKS
an imprint of Capstone Press
Mankato, Minnesota

Capstone Books are published by Capstone Press
151 Good Counsel Drive, P. O. Box 669, Mankato, Minnesota 56002
http://www.capstone-press.com

Printed in the United States of America.

Library of Congress Cataloging-in-Publication Data

Youngblood, Ed.
   Superbike Racing/by Ed Youngblood.
   p. cm. (Motorcycles)
   Includes bibliographical references (p. 45) and index.
   Summary: Traces the history of Superbike racing since its beginning in the 1970s,
describes unique features of these bikes, and indicates champion racers.
   ISBN 0-7368-0478-1
   1. Motorcycle racing—Juvenile literature. 2. Superbikes—Juvenile literature.
   [1. Motorcycle racing. 2. Motorcycles] I. Title: Superbike Racing. II. Title. III. Series.

GV1060. Y68 2000
796.75—dc21   99-053004

Editorial Credits
Blake Hoena, editor; Timothy Halldin, cover designer and illustrator; Heidi Schoof
   and Jodi Theisen, photo researchers

Photo Credits
American Motorcyclist Association, 17, 32
American Suzuki Motor Corporation, 22, 28
Archive Photos/Crady Von Pawlak, 10, 12
FPG International, 15
Index Stock Imagery/Steve Mohlen Kamp, 9
Isaac Hernandez/Mercury Press, 30
Joe Bonnello, cover, 36
Lior Rubin, 4, 7, 18, 20, 26, 34, 38, 41, 43

1 2 3 4 5 6 05 04 03 02 01 00

Table of Contents

Features

CHAPTER 1

Superbike Racing

Superbike racing is a form of motorcycle racing. It is popular in much of the world. Races are held in Europe, Japan, North America, Australia, and New Zealand. Some of these races attract audiences of more than 100,000 people. Many of the races also are televised throughout the world.

Superbike motorcycles are designed for road racing. Racers race them on paved streets or racetracks.

Superbikes are modified production-street motorcycles. These motorcycles are produced in large numbers. Companies such as Yamaha, Harley-Davidson, Ducati, and Kawasaki produce production-street motorcycles. These

Superbike racing is a form of road racing.

motorcycles are available at motorcycle dealers for the public to purchase. But racers and mechanics change these motorcycles to race them. Some of these changes make the motorcycles safe for racing. Other changes make the motorcycles' engines more powerful.

American Motorcyclist Association

The American Motorcyclist Association (AMA) began to organize motorcycle racing events in 1924. It developed superbike racing in 1976. Today, the AMA sanctions most motorcycle races in North America. Sanctioned races are official AMA racing events. These races follow AMA rules and guidelines.

The AMA sponsors both amateur and professional racing events. Amateur racers often have little or no racing experience. They do not race for money. Professional racers usually have more experience than amateur racers. They also can earn money for winning races.

The AMA works to support motorcyclists' rights and motorcycle racing. It sanctions local

The AMA sanctions most motorcycle racing events in North America.

and national races. Local races include racers from one region. National races include racers from only one country. The AMA also works with national governments to support laws that protect motorcyclists' rights. The AMA has more than 240,000 members. It even publishes its own magazine called *American Motorcyclist*.

Federation of International Motorcyclists

The Federation of International Motorcyclists (FIM) is a group of motorcycle organizations from several countries. The AMA is part of the FIM. The FIM helps racing officials organize international races. International races include racers from more than one country. The FIM sets the rules and guidelines for these races.

The FIM began to sanction superbike races shortly after the AMA developed superbike racing. Because of this, superbike racing now has a world championship title. Motorcycle racers from all over the world compete to be the Superbike World Champion.

Racers compete for this title by racing in the Superbike World Championship Series. Races in this series are held all over the world. Some of the races are run in South Africa, Spain, Italy, Germany, and the United States. Racers receive points for doing well in these races. The racer with the most points at the end of the series is the Superbike World Champion.

FIM sanctions international motorcycle racing events.

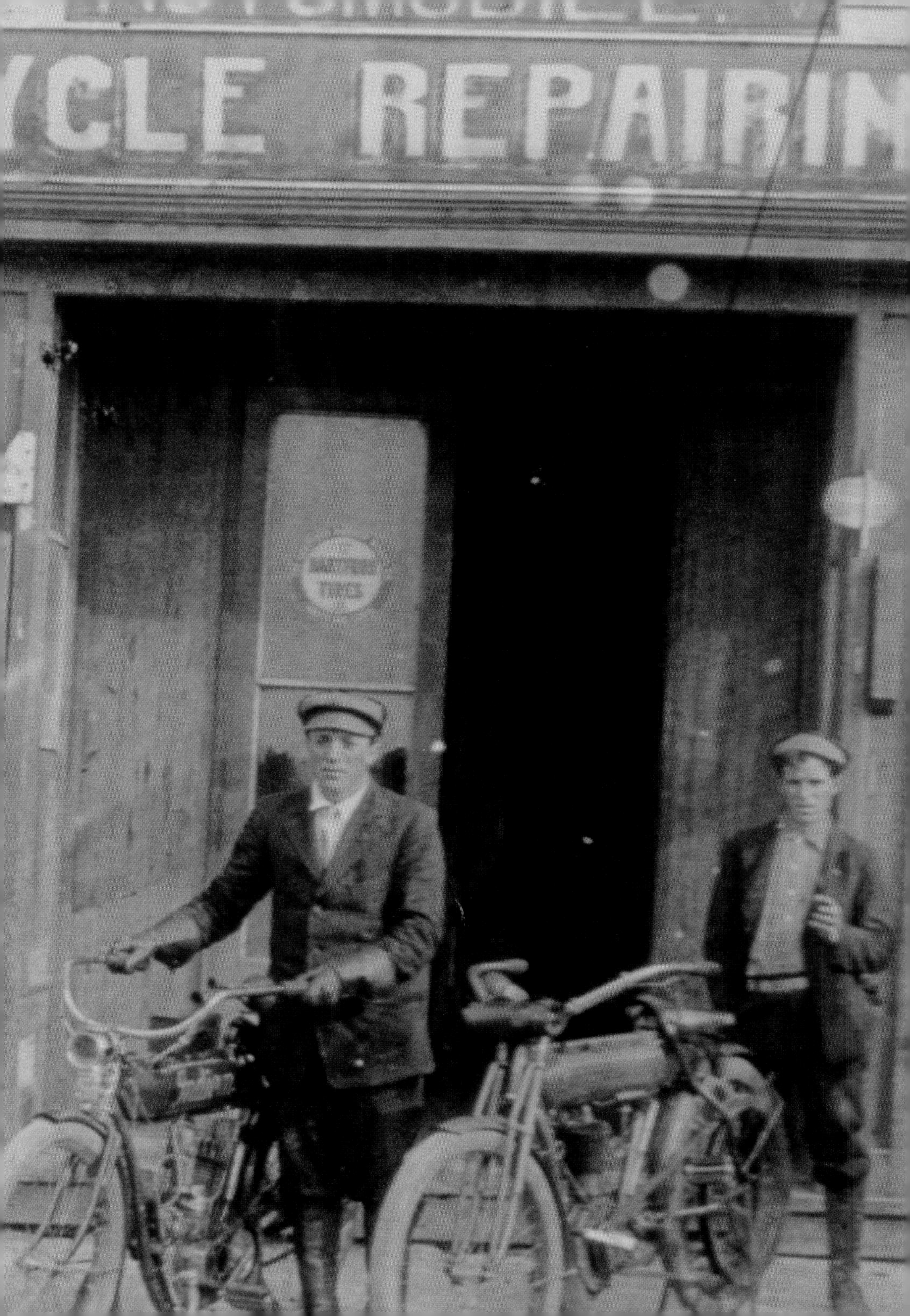
YCLE REPAIRIN

CHAPTER 2

History

In the late 1800s, European and North American inventors built the first motorcycles. Motorcycles went through many changes before the American Motorcyclist Association developed superbike racing in 1976.

The First Motorcycles

A few early motorcycle inventors attached steam-powered engines to bicycles. But these engines could be dangerous for riders. Riders often had to sit directly above the engine. Steam-powered engines gave off a great deal of heat and steam. This could burn riders.

In 1876, Nikolaus Otto invented the internal combustion engine. This engine burns fuel

Early motorcycles had engines attached to bicycles.

Harley-Davidson was one of the first important motorcycle manufacturers in North America.

inside the engine. It does not produce steam. In 1885, Gottlieb Daimler used an internal combustion engine to build a motorcycle. Gottlieb's son Paul rode this motorcycle for 10 miles (16 kilometers) around the town of Cannstatt, Germany. This proved the internal combustion engine could power motorcycles.

Motorcycle Manufacturers

By 1900, hundreds of inventors in Europe and North America built motorcycles. Before

1920, there were more than 500 motorcycle manufacturers in Europe. About 200 companies built motorcycles in North America.

Most of these motorcycles were bicycles with a small internal combustion engine attached to them. Manufacturers often left the bicycles' pedals on their motorcycles. The small motorcycle engines sometimes did not have enough power when riders drove up hills. Riders then needed to pedal to keep their motorcycles moving.

Most of the early motorcycle manufacturers quickly went out of business. They were replaced by companies that built better-designed motorcycles with more powerful engines. BSA, Triumph, Norton, and BMW were some of the important motorcycle companies in Europe. Indian, Harley-Davidson, Excelsior, Thor, and Flying Merkel were important motorcycle companies in North America.

Motorcycle Racing

Many motorcycle companies raced the motorcycles they built. Manufacturers raced their motorcycles to test new designs. Companies also used these races to show people how well their motorcycles performed. Early races took place on dirt tracks and paved public roads.

Races conducted on public roads became known as road races. Road racing was especially popular in Europe. People held large annual celebrations during certain races. These races included the Spa Francorchamps race in Belgium. They also included the races run in Brno, Czechoslovakia, and on the Isle of Man. This island is located off the coast of England. Today's motorcycle road racing world championship series grew out of these popular events.

Road Racing in the United States

Road racing did not develop as quickly in the United States as in Europe. This was because the AMA combined the results from several types of motorcycle racing events. These included road racing and dirt track racing events. Racers received points for doing well in races during the racing season. The racer with

Early motorcycle manufacturers raced their motorcycles to test new designs and advertise their motorcycles.

the most points then became the AMA Grand National Champion. The AMA's point system meant that a racer could not specialize in one type of racing. They had to be good at several types of racing to win the championship.

Before World War II (1939–1945), some of the major races in North America included both dirt and paved tracks. This was true of the

Daytona 200 in Daytona Beach, Florida. This race was 200 miles (322 kilometers) long. Racers sped down a sandy beach on one stretch of the racetrack. After this stretch, they turned a corner onto a paved public road. They then raced back to the other end of the beach.

Road racing became more popular in North America after World War II. At this time, people began buying European sports cars. These small, lightweight vehicles were fast and easy to drive on smooth, paved tracks. This also was true of European motorcycles. European motorcycles were lighter and better suited for road racing than motorcycles made in North America.

Racing officials in North America began to build special racing tracks for European cars and motorcycles. These included Sebring in Florida, Road America in Wisconsin, Laguna Seca in California, and Mosport in Ontario, Canada. People in North America became more interested in road racing when these new racetracks became available.

European motorcycles helped improve road racing in North America.

Superbike Racing

In the 1970s, the AMA created a new road racing class. This class used production-street motorcycles with 1000 cubic centimeter (cc) engines. This measurement indicates the size of a motorcycle's engine. Many companies built motorcycles with 1000cc engines. These companies included Ducati, Moto Guzzi, BMW, Suzuki, Kawasaki, and Honda. AMA

Motorcycle manufacturers took more interest in road racing when it was given its own championship titles.

officials believed that more people had an opportunity to race because of the availability of these motorcycles.

At first, this racing class was called production racing. In 1976, the AMA created a national championship title for this racing class. They then called this class superbikes. Reg Pridmore of Goleta, California, became the first superbike national champion. He rode a BMW motorcycle. Pridmore became the champion again in 1977 and 1978. During these years, he rode a Kawasaki motorcycle.

Also in 1976, the AMA abandoned the old Grand National Championship points system. This system made racers earn points in both road and dirt track racing events. This system favored dirt track racers because more dirt track races were held each year. Road racing became more important when it was given its own championship titles.

Motorcycle manufacturers took a greater interest in road racing with this change. They began to sponsor factory teams for road racing. Manufacturers hire racers to race for these teams. These racers then use the manufacturers' motorcycles and equipment.

Superbike Engines

Superbike racers ride motorcycles with two to four cylinders. The cylinder is the space inside an engine where gasoline is burned to create power. European manufacturers mostly built

Japanese manufacturers put a great deal of effort into developing fast and powerful four-cylinder motorcycles.

two-cylinder motorcycles. Japanese motorcycle manufacturers mainly built four-cylinder motorcycles.

Japanese motorcycle manufacturers put a great deal of effort into the development of their superbikes. Japanese motorcycles soon became much faster and more powerful than European two-cylinder motorcycles.

In 1982, the AMA changed superbike racing rules. The AMA wanted to keep more motorcycle manufacturers involved in superbike racing. Engine size and the number of cylinders in an engine help determine how much power the engine creates. Four-cylinder superbikes are now limited to 750cc engines. Three-cylinder motorcycles can have 900cc engines. Two-cylinder motorcycles still can use 1000cc engines. This rule has produced more even competition between motorcycle manufacturers.

Popularity of Superbike Racing

With the new rules, superbike racing became popular throughout the world. By 1987, superbikes had become the most important motorcycle road racing class in North America. In 1988, the Federation of International Motorcyclists created the Superbike World

Superbikes can reach speeds of more than 180 miles (290 kilometers) per hour.

Championship Series. U.S. racers won the world championship five of the first six years.

Superbikes are modified production-street motorcycles. The popularity of superbike racing caused changes in street motorcycle designs. By 1980, superbike owners had learned how to modify their motorcycles' engines. These changes allowed them to produce more power from their motorcycles' engines. The modified engines were able to produce as much as 150 horsepower. This unit of measurement measures an engine's power. These modified engines produced twice the horsepower that most motorcycles were designed to produce.

The frames of these motorcycles were not designed to support this much power. Early superbikes were hard to handle and difficult to steer at racing speeds. These speeds could reach as high as 180 miles (290 kilometers) per hour. The motorcycles were so powerful that their frames sometimes shook at these speeds.

Sports Bikes

In 1983, Honda became the first company to design a street motorcycle intended for superbike racing. The motorcycle was the VF750 Interceptor.

The VF750 had all the parts required for a street-legal motorcycle. Riders need this equipment to be allowed to drive their motorcycles on public roads. This equipment includes mirrors, lights, mufflers, and turn signals. But the VF750 also had streamlined bodywork similar to racing motorcycles. This plastic covering over a motorcycle's engine was built to have less wind resistance at high speeds. Wind resistance is a force of air that opposes movement. The VF750 even had a new frame design strong enough to support a more powerful engine.

The VF750 Interceptor started a trend that changed motorcycle manufacturing throughout the world. Other manufacturers built new race-designed motorcycles. Kawasaki produced its ZX series motorcycles. Suzuki made GSXR motorcycles. These motorcycles are called sport bikes. Sport bikes are painted with bright colors and patterns similar to racing motorcycles. Sport bikes are built with engine sizes ranging from 250cc to 1100cc. Manufacturers build these motorcycles for people who want their motorcycles to look like racing motorcycles. But most of these people do not intend to race.

Champions

World Superbike Champions
1999 Carl Fogerty, Great Britain
1998 Carl Fogerty, Great Britain
1997 John Kocinski, USA
1996 Troy Corser, Australia
1995 Carl Fogerty, Great Britain
1994 Carl Fogerty, Great Britain
1993 Scott Russell, USA
1992 Doug Polen, USA
1991 Doug Polen, USA
1990 Raymond Roche, France

AMA Superbike Champions
1999 Mathew Mladin, Australia
1998 Ben Bostrom, California
1997 Doug Chandler, California
1996 Doug Chandler, California
1995 Miguel Duhamel, Quebec
1994 Troy Corser, Australia
1993 Doug Polen, Texas
1992 Scott Russell, Georgia
1991 Thomas Stevens, Florida
1990 Doug Chandler, California

CHAPTER 3

Equipment

Motorcycles used in superbike competitions must be approved by the AMA and the FIM. Their engines must be the proper size for the superbike class. The motorcycles also must be based on production-street models. Motorcycles are considered production-street models when the motorcycle manufacturer has produced at least 150 of them.

Modifications
Racers modify their superbikes once the brand of superbike they use is approved for racing. These changes include removing street equipment that is not needed to race. This includes lights, mirrors, and turn signals.

Superbikes are modified production-street motorcycles.

The fairing is the bodywork of a motorcycle.

The exhaust system also can be modified to improve engine performance. Superbikes must have mufflers. Mufflers decrease engine noise. But superbike mufflers can be about 20 decibels louder than street motorcycles. Sound is measured in decibels.

A production-street motorcycle's fairing is usually made of plastic. The fairing covers the motorcycle's engine and front end. It can be replaced with a carbon-fiber fairing for racing. Carbon fiber is a much stronger and lighter material than plastic. But the basic shape of the original fairing cannot be changed.

Racers can change their superbike's engine to increase the engine's power. Modern superbike racing engines produce 160 to 170 horsepower. This is about 50 horsepower more than similar, unmodified street-production motorcycles.

No major changes can be made to the superbike's frame. The frame's dimensions must be the same as the original model. Material can be added to the frame to make it stronger or to improve the motorcycle's handling. But the motorcycle must weigh no less than 355 pounds (161 kilograms).

The rider's controls must remain unchanged. These include the throttle, front and rear brakes, and the clutch. The throttle serves the same purpose as a car's gas pedal and controls the motorcycle's speed. The clutch allows

Factory teams often travel in tractor trailers.

racers to shift gears on their motorcycle. Motorcycles travel faster in higher gears.

Superbike Teams
Honda, Suzuki, Kawasaki, Yamaha, Ducati, and Harley-Davidson sponsor factory teams in AMA superbike racing. All of these companies except Harley-Davidson also sponsor teams in the World Superbike Championship Series.

Factory teams travel to races in motor coaches or tractor trailers. These trucks are painted colorfully and help advertise the names of the companies. But their main purpose is to carry motorcycles and parts. They also contain repair shops and living quarters for racers.

Tires

Tire selection is an important factor to winning a superbike race. Superbikes use tires that look different than street-motorcycle tires. Superbike tires have no tread. They are smooth and made of soft rubber. The soft rubber gives the tires better traction to grip pavement.

Racing tires are designed to operate at very high temperatures. Tires heat up when they rub against pavement. The minimum operating temperature for racing tires is 212 degrees Fahrenheit (100 degrees Celsius). This is the temperature of boiling water. But this temperature is still too low for good racing tire performance. The best operating temperature for racing tires is 239 degrees Fahrenheit (115 degrees Celsius). Tires that approach 266

Superbikes use smooth tires made of soft rubber.

degrees Fahrenheit (130 degrees Celsius) will
begin to fall apart. When this happens, racers
may have to slow down to let the tires cool.

Racing teams use tire heaters to warm up
their motorcycle's tires before a race. Tire
heaters look like electric blankets. Racers wrap
these heaters around their motorcycle's tires.
Racing at full speed on cool tires will cause
the tires to blister or break apart. During some

races, racers are allowed to drive around the track before the race starts. This also helps the tires to heat up.

Racing teams sometimes fill tires with nitrogen. This gas keeps tires at a more consistent pressure during temperature changes. Nitrogen does not expand or contract as much as air does during temperature changes.

Pit Stops

The Daytona 200 is the only superbike race in North America where racers make pit stops. During pit stops, racing teams change tires, make necessary repairs, and fill the gas tank.

Racers make pit stops at Daytona 200 because the race is longer than other national championship races. Most of these races are about 50 miles (80 kilometers) long. Superbike racing tires wear out after about 50 miles. The Daytona 200 is 200 miles (322 kilometers) long.

Safety Equipment

Superbike racing can be dangerous. Racers speed around the track at more than 100 miles (161 kilometers) per hour. They often race

Pucks on racers' knees slide smoothly along the pavement when racers lean into turns.

within inches (centimeters) of one another. When racers lean into turns, their knees may drag across the pavement. Safety rules and proper protection are very important.

Racers must wear full-coverage helmets. A full-coverage helmet covers a racer's entire head. This includes the face and jaw. Some of these helmets have fins on top to make them cut smoothly through the air. These fins help prevent racers' heads from being shaken or thrown about by the wind.

Racers also wear custom-made leather suits. Leather is tough and helps prevent injuries. These suits also contain padding and hard plastic body armor at the elbows, knees, hips, and shoulders. On the outside of each knee is a puck. This piece of hard nylon slides smoothly on the pavement when riders lean into turns. Riders also wear a flexible plastic back protector under their suit. They wear gloves and boots. The helmets, suits, boots, and gloves often are colorful. They display the names and logos of some of the rider's sponsors.

A superbike's fairing is designed both for speed and safety. It is streamlined to reduce wind resistance at high speeds. AMA rules require fairings to have a container at the bottom. This container catches oil if the motorcycle's engine explodes. This will prevent oil from spilling onto the track. Oil spills can cause other racers to crash.

Doug Chandler

Birth Date: September 27, 1965
Home Town: Salinas, California
Turned Professional: 1983

AMA Superbike Rankings
1999 – 4th
1998 – 2nd
1997 – 1st
1996 – 1st
1995 – 15th
1990 – 1st
1989 – 5th
1988 – 3rd
1987 – 5th

Doug Chandler began his motorcycle racing career on dirt tracks. In 1983, he started racing professionally. That same year he also was "Dirt Track Rookie of the Year." Chandler was considered the best first-year professional racer that year. He started road racing in 1984. Chandler started superbike racing in 1987. In 1989, Chandler won his first superbike race at the Mid-Ohio Sports Car Course in Lexington, Ohio. In 1999, he had three wins and is currently racing for Muzzy Kawasaki team.

CHAPTER 4

Safety and Skills

Nearly 700 men and women are licensed by the AMA for professional motorcycle road racing. The AMA licenses racers to make sure they have the needed skills for road racing. It can be difficult to control motorcycles at speeds of more than 180 miles (290 kilometers) per hour.

Racers must be at least 16 years old to receive a professional racing license. They also must qualify to earn a professional racing license by first racing in amateur races.

Fewer than 250 professional racers hold a license to race superbikes. To earn this license, racers must race for a year in another class of professional motorcycle road racing.

Almost 250 professional racers are licensed by the AMA to race superbikes.

Miguel Duhamel from LaSalle, Quebec is one of the top AMA superbike racers today. Miguel has won more than 20 superbike races. Miguel was the AMA National Superbike Champion in 1995. His father, Yvon Duhamel, also was a champion road racer in the 1970s.

Fred Merkel from Fountain Valley, California, is one of the best superbike racers of all time. Merkel had 20 superbike victories in the United States. He earned half of those in 1984. He became the AMA Superbike National Champion in 1984, 1985, and 1986. In 1987, he moved to Italy to compete in the World Superbike Championship. He won the World Superbike Championship in both 1988 and 1989.

Flags and Lights

During races, officials use lights or flags to advise racers about safety conditions. A green flag or light starts the race. During the race, officials show yellow flags or lights for minor hazards such as oil spills. Racers are not allowed to pass one another during these caution signals. Officials may bring out a

Officials may show a yellow light or wave a yellow flag during accidents.

pace car if something serious happens during the race such as an accident. When this happens, the racers line up behind the pace car. It then escorts them slowly around the track until the hazardous situation is corrected.

During very serious conditions, officials may show a red light or wave red flags. This signal means the race has been stopped. A red flag or light may be used during rain.

A black flag means a racer must leave the track. Officials usually wave this flag when there is something wrong with a racer's motorcycle. It may be spilling oil or a part may be loose.

Officials also use other flags to signal racers. A light blue flag with a yellow stripe means that a racer is about to be passed by a faster racer. Green and white flags held in a cross mean that the race is half over. A white flag means there is only one lap left in the race. A checkered flag means the race is over. The first racer who crosses the finish line as the checkered flag is being waved is the winner.

Track Racing Advisory Committee

Safety has become more important as road racing motorcycles have become faster. In 1998, the AMA formed the Track Racing Advisory Committee (TRAC) to help improve racetrack safety. TRAC is made up of race officials, professional racers, and racing team managers. TRAC members meet with racetrack owners. They help owners find affordable ways to make their tracks safer for motorcycle racing.

The Track Racing Advisory Committee helps improve motorcycle safety.

Words to Know

amateur (AM-uh-chur)—a racer who does not earn money for racing

clutch (KLUHCH)—a lever that allows riders to shift gears on their motorcycles

cylinder (SIL-uhn-dur)—the space in an internal combustion engine where fuel is burned to create power

horsepower (HORSS-pou-ur)—the measure of an engine's power

internal combustion engine (in-TUR-nuhl kuhm-BUSS-chuhn EN-juhn)—an engine that creates power by burning gasoline inside

professional (pruh-FESH-uh-nuhl)—a racer who can earn money for racing

sanction (SANGK-shuhn)—to officially approve of a race

throttle (THROT-uhl)—a device drivers use to control the speed of their vehicle

To Learn More

Dregni, Michael. *Motorcycle Racing.* MotorSports. Mankato, Minn: Capstone Books, 1994.

Jay, Jackson. *Motorcycles.* Rollin'. Mankato, Minn.: Capstone Books, 1996.

Ryder, Julian. *World Superbikes: The First Ten Years.* Newbury Park, Calif.: Haynes, 1997.

Webster, Charlie and Mike Morris. *Superbikes.* Hauppauge, N.Y.: Barron's, 1996.

Useful Addresses

American Motorcyclist Association
13515 Yarmouth Drive
Pickerington, OH 43147

Canadian Motorcycle Association
P.O. Box 448
Hamilton, ON L8L 1J4
Canada

Federation of International Motorcyclists
11 Route Suisse
CH-1295 MIES
Switzerland

Internet Sites

American Motorcyclist Association
http://www.ama-cycle.org

Canadian Motorcycle Association
http://www.canmocycle.ca

Federation of International Motorcyclists
http://www.fim.ch

SBK '99
http://www.superbike.it

Index